FENG
SH * T

The Art of Domestic Disorder

D1370001

FENG SH * T

The Art of Domestic Disorder

ANNA CROSBIE

UNIVERSE

First published in the United States of America in 2002
by Universe Publishing
A Division of Rizzoli International Publications, Inc.
300 Park Avenue South
New York, NY 10010
©2002 by Universe Publishing

Originally published in 2001 by Boxtree
an imprint of Pan Macmillan Ltd
Pan Macmillan, 20 New Wharf Road, London N1 9RR
Basingstoke and Oxford
Copyright © Anna Crosbie 2001

2002 2003 2004 2005/3 5 7 9 8 6 4 2

Design by Dan Newman/Perfect Bound Ltd
Manufactured in Hong Kong, PRC
Library of Congress Control Number: 2001099689
ISBN: 0-7893-0679-4

Domestic Disorder *n.* a state of dirty or unpleasant untidiness.

Instead of rearranging stuff in your house to improve your inner harmony (or whatever), try the equally ancient art of Feng Sh*t. This definitive guide is packed with simple and practical tips, and will change your life forever! (It will certainly change the lives of those you live with ...)

EENIE MEENIE MINIE MO

Aim to have at least six different bottles of
shampoo and conditioner open and
in use at any one time.

LET THEM DO IT

A key advantage of married life is the
fifty per cent reduction in your obligation
to change the sheets.

MALODOROUS MESS

Never wash out your cans properly before you
put them in the recycling. This way they will
start to smell quite nicely within a few days.

CREATING BALANCE IN YOUR ENVIRONMENT

Use the top shelf of the closet to build a
structurally challenged pile of things
you might one day either throw away
or store in the attic.

NO CLEAN CUPS?

Purchase extra supplies of mugs, teaspoons, and knives. They will equip you to survive an extra day before having to do the dishes.

THE PHYSICS OF
MAXIMUM DAMP

Remember that towels dry better hanging
horizontally.

POTTED PLANTS

Kill them. Leave them in situ for six months
before burial.

YOUR VACATION UNPACKING FORMULA

$$\frac{x\,(x+2)}{3} = y$$

x = the number of days you were on vacation

y = the number of days you leave your half-unpacked suitcases and toiletry bags scattered throughout the house

HAVE A 'THINGS PENDING' WALL

Bookshelves make an ideal holding pen
for miscellaneous chores–items, for example,
you intend to file some day, return to the
store for a refund, fix, or mail to
your cousin in Wisconsin.

WHEN THE PAPER
RUNS OUT . . .

Leave empty toilet paper rolls
on the bathroom floor.
They will eventually make their
own way to the trash can.

FLOWER POWER

Keep bouquets in their vases long enough
to ensure that the leaves and petals drop
onto the floor.

DISH MOUNTAIN

"This needs soaking" is a Feng Sh*t mantra.
Use and abuse it.

IN HONOR AND MEMORY
OF THY MISSING LIDS

Religion is an important cornerstone of
Feng Sh*t. Make your bathroom windowsill
a shrine to capless tubes of toothpaste.

COFFEE TABLES

Buy one designed to display lavish, oversized photography books. Use the lower shelf to create an 8ft^2 living sculpture called *I Think My Lost Car Keys Are In There Somewhere*.

FENG FRIDGE

Cover your refrigerator door with magnets, memos, alphabet sets, shopping lists, favorite postcards, and cartoons. This will replace a clean, white empty surface with a random visual explosion–Feng Sh*t at its finest.

FEE FI FO FENG

Growing seeds is such fun! Nurture some herbs on your windowsill in little terracotta pots. The herbs won't grow and the soil will become damp and moldy. If you're lucky some spiders might move in, or a cigarette butt.

ELIMINATE GRATUITOUS CHORES

The bathtub sees more fresh water than
any other household object or surface.
It is therefore self-cleaning.

PETS

Long-haired varieties are best.
(Though parakeets and camels are also good.)

THE MODERN ELEMENT

Fire, Earth, Wind, and Water are all
fine and dandy, but devotees
of Feng Sh*t prefer Plastic!
Save supermarket shopping bags as
if your life depended on it.

NEWSPAPERS

Buy the Sunday paper every weekend. Leave it scattered all over the table until you read it on Saturday. Leave the supplements in the bathroom until someone else removes them.

PENS

Never, EVER throw one out.

PILE & DUMP

Use piles to collect and store dirty laundry. Studies show that beneath the door of the washing machine, at the foot of your bed, and any spot on the bathroom floor work best.

BABIES

Have as many as possible.

TOYS

Only buy huge toys, made of garish, primary-colored pieces of plastic.

"I'M DAMNED IF I'M PICKING THAT UP!"

Make this phrase your mantra. Toys with zillions of pieces are also good; try large tubs of LEGO and little wooden train sets.

WHEN YOU DON'T KNOW
WHERE ELSE TO PUT IT

Place a large bowl next to the telephone as an exclusive home for your keys. Fill the bowl instead with not-sure-if-these-are-used-or-not batteries, paper clips, coupons, phone cards, some staples, one shoelace, a screwdriver, nail clippers, three stamps, a box of matches, and a broken doorknob.

CHILDREN

Tell them that being messy is cool.
Tell them they are responsible for
making their own mess.

BORROW THEM IF
YOU HAVE TO

If you don't have babies or young children
of your own, it helps to have someone
else's visit once in a while.

CABINETS

Are not for storing things. They are
for hiding things.

WARNING! COULD BE TIDY IF
MANAGED BETTER

Never put CDs back in their correct cases.
This will create hours of fun for your
anally-retentive loved one.

FENG LAUNDRY No. 1

1) Leave clean laundry in a pile (somewhere) to await folding.

2) Leave pile so long that you retrieve and wear most of it before you fold it.

3) Throw the remnants of the clean pile back into the laundry basket.

IRONING

Don't provide your iron and ironing board
with a permanent home. This ensures they
will be constantly up and visible, somewhere.

CLUTTER

One can never own too many
coasters or throw pillows.

FENG SH*T FOR LIFE

The mail is a free Feng Sh*t Ingredient.
Send away for just one catalog and
as if by magic your name will appear
on every junk-mail list in the country.

I WONDER WHAT
THIS GOES TO?

When in doubt, keep it. One never knows
when the World Screw Shortage Crisis will
kick in.

VACUUMING

Vacuuming is just silly: don't do it.

BUT IF YOU MUST . . .

Vacuum just one or two rooms, then leave
the vacuum cleaner out in a *really annoying*
place, on the pretence that you will finish
the other rooms later.

. . . AND BE STUPID ABOUT IT

Vacuuming is more fun if you never empty the
dust bag.

THE HIDDEN BENEFIT OF RECYCLING

It is more auspicious to have large or high objects behind your house rather than in the front. On hearing this some people might run off to plant a hedge. But disciples of Feng Sh*t know it's much easier and cheaper just to stack your recycling boxes (a.k.a. ninety-three glass jars and bottles and seventeen tons of newspapers) at the *rear* of your house.

VERTICAL PILING

Every home needs a bulletin board. If you
need some ideas for things to put on it (and
we're sure you won't), try menus, eclectic
business cards, expired supermarket coupons,
inspirational recipes, and mystery phone
numbers. Cull the contents only when
you run out of thumb tacks.

PHOTO OVERLOAD

Every time you develop a roll of film, get
doubles. Leave your favorite two or three
snapshots propped up on the nearest shelf.

BELIEVE IN THE AFTERLIFE

Convince yourself that all household odds and
ends should be saved for future use (one is
bound to present itself one day). Accordingly,
hoard buttons, string, and twist ties
with conviction.

BREED PURSES

Operate several purses at the same time. Have different ones for work, formal, and casual occasions. Let them all hang out in different rooms as they wait for their next outing.

SAVOR THE FLAVOR

Retain used coffee grounds in the bottom of
your filter for a minimum of two days.

BUBBLE WRAP

An endangered species! Save all used bubble
wrap regardless of how much you already
have saved and how little space you have
in which to store it.

ALLOW YOUR PETS TO SCAVENGE

Pets that scavenge are more likely to deposit the following on your carpets: remnants of dead, small, furry or fluffy critters; mud and soil samples from recent expeditions; and a selection of local leaves, grasses, cobwebs, and insect wings.

DON'T BE ASHAMED

Remember that dishwashers are for storing
dirty dishes as well as cleaning them.

GET MORE CLUTTER

Knick-knacks can be squeezed into the
smallest of spaces. The more you have,
the less appealing dusting will be.

LIVE BY LOGIC

The following are happiest living on the kitchen counter—never put them away:

the can opener

the plastic wrap

the aspirin

your sunglasses

STORAGE SYSTEMS

Are great! You still won't put things away.

1. The rattan boxes for which you've paid a fortune will remain mostly empty.

2. Meanwhile they will add a whole new stratum of clutter to the room.

HAVE USELESS AIDS

Buy one of the many absolutely useless mops
available these days. Then when you do mop
the floor, it won't look any cleaner anyway.

THE LAYERED LOOK

Exploit the drying potential of every
radiator, door knob, and towel bar.

CHAIRS

Were made for hanging
coats on.

ACCEPT DEFEAT

Don't bother trying to figure out how used
teabags might make it to the trash can
without dripping all over the floor.

OUR FAVORITE INVENTION

Buy a duvet. Duvet owners never
need to make the bed.

SPRING

Is for daffodil picking, the consumption of
chocolate bunnies, and afternoon walks
without your hat and scarf. *Spring Cleaning*
is in fact a keep-active-therapy for people
in need of a life.

BEDROOM POSITIONS

Placing your bed in the corner of the bedroom
diagonally opposite the entrance is auspicious.
Sleeping with your head toward the east
maximizes the flow of *chi* and will ensure
restful nights.

But most important . . .
placing a large armchair directly adjacent to
your closet means you'll never have to put
your clothes away again.

THE DOOR MAT

Never use it.

PETS HAVE FEELINGS, TOO

Make sure their feeding bowls are inside.

THE FRUIT BOWL

Put your new, fresh fruit on top of old fruit
that will decay imminently.

FENG SHOES

Just let them park and rest
wherever they want to.

DE RIGUEUR

These things you *must* own! They have a Feng Sh*t capability all of their own and will require little effort on your part:

Sofa throws

Socks

Bath mats

Soap holders

SIZE DOES MATTER

Buy a very small bedside table, with barely
enough surface space for a lamp. Your alarm
clock, tissues, book, glasses, and pajamas
will have to colonize the carpet instead.
Left to their own devices they will lay
claim to territory under the bed, too.

I'LL DEAL WITH THAT LATER . . .

Leave all mail scattered for at least one week
in the place where you first opened it.

. . . IF I CAN FIND IT

Never put today's mail in the same place as
yesterday's.

DIY . . .

Never finish what you start . . .

. . . MEANS "DONE IT YET?"

Leave your hammers, tape measures, paint brushes, and stepladder lying around until you do finish.

No. 1 PUBLIC ENEMIES

The most virulent Feng Sh*t efforts can be rapidly undermined by the effects of these enemy agents:

The smell of furniture polish

Martha Stewart

Impending visits from your mother-in-law

Beware and avoid if you can.

FENG FOOD

Avoid sitting at the table to eat or drink.
This makes it easier to leave mugs by the side
of the bath, cereal bowls on the bedroom
floor, and the salt and pepper next to the sofa.

HAVE MULTIPLE WEALTH CORNERS

Reserve a flat surface area in every room for dumping loose change.

A BIG ISSUE

Cobwebs are the intricate and sophisticated labor of love of helpless and minuscule creatures. They are also their home. Leave them alone.

NON-MAINTENANCE

Delay the replacement of broken light bulbs.
Their lack of function will heighten your
home's general ambience of indifference.

CREATE FUTURE
ARCHAEOLOGY

Preserve in your bathroom cabinet every
lipstick and nail polish you
have ever owned.

BACK PORCHES

Don't have one. Your muddy boots, wet
umbrellas, collapsed strollers, and other
sundries will be forced to create havoc
elsewhere in the house.

MOST EASILY SULLIED
SURFACES AWARDS

1st Prize to cream carpets.

2nd Prize to tiles with deep grouting.

3rd Prize to sisal rugs.

HO HO HOARD

The Christmas season provides fertile
Feng Sh*t fodder. Start hoarding piles of
gift wrap, decorations, presents and
edibles in September.

CHRISTMAS TIDYINGS

Get a real Christmas tree with guaranteed
vacuum-proof needle drop.

THIS ONE'S DEAD SIMPLE

Don't bother donating unwanted clothes and household knick-knacks to charity. Keep everything. When you die your relatives will give it to a charity shop for you.

FUNCTION 1
PRETENTIOUSNESS

The mantelpiece aspires to be a grand architectural feature. Such aspirations are easy to quash. Use yours as a functional shelf on which to store wedding invites, old postcards, champagne corks, a bowl of stale peanuts, fourteen different candles, and the VCR manual.

* @\ * # ~ * **POTS!!**

If treated properly, pot carousels can be a
useless storage solution and a brilliant
Feng Sh*t aid. Make sure you have at least
one in your kitchen. Create an impenetrable
mass of pots, lids, graters, tins, and trays;
it will evolve into an unstoppable cascade
each time you try to use it.

BATHING ACCESSORIES

Austerity need not apply to modern bathing conditions. Surround your bath with the leisure accessories of your dreams–loofahs, inflatable pillows, jars of bath salts, and floating candles, for example. Watch them increase the surface space available to mildew and various bath scums.

SAVE MONEY WHILST
CREATING HOUSE MESS

Buy in bulk! The gigantic boxes of detergent, multi-packs of kitchen towels and the oversized box of Rice Krispies® will be too big to fit on your shelves. You'll have to leave them out in a really impractical and conspicuous place.

WE ♥ CRUMBS!

Place your toaster where it can be most
easily knocked.

BRING YOUR INSIDE OUTSIDE

Your garden is but an additional room of
your house. Treat it accordingly, and leave
it to grow in whichever state and style of
Sh*t it prefers.

GET SUSTAINABLE!

Start a compost heap and keep a scraps bowl
by the kitchen sink. There is something very
risqué about decomposing vegetables.

I'M BORED OF THIS NOW

Constantly start new hobbies and
quickly learn to dislike them. Their
incomplete creations make a unique
breed of Feng Sh*t.

WORK FROM HOME!

1. Create an office in
an inadequate corner of an unsuitable room.

2. Stack an inappropriate amount of computer
paper, envelopes, and fax paper on an
inadequately sized shelf.

3. The rest will take care of itself.

OFFICE FILING SYSTEM

Don't have one.

BAN CABINET CLEANING

Ignore expiration dates. The most fertile
breeding grounds for superfluous objects are
spice racks, baking cupboards,
and medicine cabinets.

THE BLACK HOLE

You need only consider your oven's cleanliness when its use triggers off all smoke alarms and the billowing by-products of its caked interior threatens to asphyxiate you. You then have two options:

1. Get in an industrial cleaning service for a day.

2. Buy a new oven.

DUPLICATE

Don't throw out last year's editions of the
phone directory and Yellow Pages when the
new ones are delivered.

MAGAZINE RACKS

The more you own, the more compelled you'll
be to keep ridiculous quantities of obsolete
and trashy magazines.

GET FIT & FANATICAL

Buy an abdominal cruncher and an exercise
bike. Regardless of how often or not you
use them, you will never fold them up for
storage, and you will eventually succumb
to their suitability for the hanging
or drying of clothes.

HAT TRICK AWARD

Have an open fire. They necessitate three

of the finest Feng Sh*t attributes yet

discovered by man:

Kindling

Wood baskets

Ash

ENCOURAGEMENT

Three simple reasons to adopt Feng Sh*t as a
lifestyle choice:

- more time to eat

- more time to drink

- more time to sleep

FLAUNT YOUR ACHIEVEMENTS

The molding and trim in the bathroom are easily scrutinized by visiting eyes. For the maximum promotion of your Feng Sh*t abilities, ensure they are the last surface to be cleaned of dirt, grime, and cobwebs.

INEVITABLE MESS

Windows + Condensation = MILDEW

(White or cream curtains
display mildew best.)

COAT RACKS

Are for the permanent storage of old coats
you will never wear again.

THE "CRAM IT ALL IN" THEOREM

Fill the cabinet under the kitchen sink with three times more Tupperware containers, rubbish bags, light bulbs, and shoe polish than should ever physically fit. Select items will then fall onto the floor with joyous, reckless abandon every time you open the door.

HUNT & GATHER

Scavenge shells, pebbles, and other natural items for display in the bathroom. They will collect dust, possibly mold, and won't look anything like those in the "Design Ideas for Your Home" article that inspired you.

GET SENTIMENTAL

Dry that special bunch of roses and hang it upside down with a ribbon. It will warm the cockles of your heart with its associated memories, while handily looking to others like just more junk.

THIS LITTLE PIGGY

Had toenails that went "Wee Wee Wee!"
all over the carpet, or the bathroom floor tiles,
or the sheets.

GYM CLOTHES THEOREM

Degree of
Clothes'
Dampness
& Odor

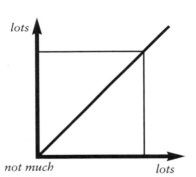

Time it takes to remove clothes from
gym bag and place in laundry basket

OVEN MITTS

Are designed to hang neatly on the oven rail.
Ensure your oven door is permanently stuffed
with surplus dish towels, and there will never
be room for your oven mitts.
See how easy this is?

MEN CAN DO IT, TOO

Men are reminded that disposable razors do not by nature of their name require immediate disposal. Keep up to twenty used ones in or around the toothbrush holder.

VEGETABLE PUEEEEW!

Did you know that if you store your potatoes and onions in the same vegetable rack, the onions will emit a chemical that makes your potatoes spoil faster?

You do now!

HARMONIZING YOUR INNER & OUTER SPACES

Keep stale bread *inside* your bread box, and fresh bread *outside* your bread box.

GIDDY UP!

The drying rack
was surely invented by a fanatical
Feng Sh*t devotee!
Use one all year round.

SHOW OFF

Running out of ideas for new house clutter?
Hunt out any old academic, hobby or sporting
related medals and trophies, and make a mini-
shrine to your youthful talent.

COAT HANGERS

Are another household item with a
predisposed, genetic inclination to roam
freely between all rooms of your house.
When the sales clerk says "Would you
like the hanger with that?" always answer,
"Yes, please!"

LEAVE YOUR WORK STRESS
NEAR THE DOOR

It is important to relax when you get home
from work. Take off your tie or scarf as soon
as you get in the door and discard it over the
nearest (vacant) chair back.

YOUR VERY OWN ELECTRIC COMPANY

Dedicate a lone electrical socket around which the rechargers and cords for all the mobile phones in your house can entwine.

THE FUN YOU CAN HAVE WITH A CLOSE-UP PHOTO OF PUPPIES (DISSECTED INTO 500 PIECES)!

Allocate a corner of your dining table
for your jigsaw puzzle, and take a
very long time to finish it.

LIVE WITH AS MANY WOMEN AS POSSIBLE

Through their ownership of make-up, perfumes, hair sprays and gels, styling combs and brushes, and hair ties and accessories, women have a significantly greater statistical probability of destroying the bathroom.

TWO INTO ONE WON'T GO

Own twice as many utensils as there are
hooks on your kitchen utensil rack.

TWO INTO ONE WON'T GO #2

Own twice as many mugs as there are
available cup hooks or mug tree spaces.

POINTS FOR EFFORT

A matching set of pretty labeled containers is an ideal present for dedicated servants of Feng Sh*t. You know the sort: "Tea," "Coffee," "Flour," "Pasta," "Brown Sugar." Arrange them neatly in your kitchen and fill them with completely unrelated contents.

THE POWER OF PROCRASTINATION

Where possible, buy clothes that require hand washing. They will linger in your laundry for considerably longer than machine-washable items and take twice as long to dry.

SHENG CHI

This is good chi: *a positive energy that flows in a meandering fashion.*
Make it by leaving your briefcase, sports bag, or whatever else is necessary on pertinent areas of the floor, so that the most direct routes between rooms are obstructed.
Meander past.

ANY OLD EXCUSE

Shar chi is bad energy.
Sharp, spiky things create *Shar chi*.
What a perfect reason to permanently
avoid your broom.

IT COULD BE YOU

Be very lax about checking your lottery
tickets, then you will feel obliged to keep all
of them until they become out of date.

I KNOW I HAD IT
SOMEWHERE . . .

Just in case they contain a telephone number
or address you might need one day, keep all
your office and personal diaries from the
previous five years.

WHAT IS DEWEY DECIMAL ANYWAY?

A subtle but effective Feng Sh*t tip . . .
Take any vertical, straight or parallel rows of
books off your bookshelf, and replace them in
random, leaning, and perpendicular piles.

SLOPPY ADMINISTRATION HELPS

Leave all the faxes you have received or sent in the past few weeks lying beside, under, or on top of your fax machine.

BONUS: Not only will this increase your Domestic Disorder, it will really irritate other fax users.

"CAN'T DO IT PROPERLY SO THAT WILL GODDAMN DO"

Install lots of Venetian blinds in your house. Evidence shows that most men are unable to operate a Venetian blind, and their endearing attempts to do so will leave your curtains looking suitably disarranged.

TEN GREEN BOTTLES

To compensate for the cleaning up you were forced to do for Saturday night's dinner party, leave the numerous empty wine and beer bottles it generated in a pile on the kitchen floor for at least a week.

BUT IT'S WHAT MY MOTHER USED TO DO

If your dinner party leaves you with some half-full wine bottles, cork the reds and keep them on the kitchen counter because leftover red wine is perfect to put in a big pot of lamb stew (not that you've ever, in your entire life, made lamb stew).

QUITE SIMPLY . . .

Life is *too* short to clean under rugs . . .

. . . FORGET IT!

. . . or behind large appliances.

RAISE THE STAKES

Every so often, forget to put your trash out
for the garbage men.

ARE THEY STILL ALL RIGHT
TO EAT?

Wait for someone else to throw out
the two stale cookies in the
bottom of the box.

THE REAL INDICATOR OF YOUR FENG SH*T COMMITMENT

The fact that your linen closet isn't seen by
visitors is no excuse for keeping it tidy.

MAXIMIZE ALL CLEANABLE SURFACE AREAS

When choosing paintings and prints, remember that thick, deep frames will catch more dust and cobwebs.

MMM, I SHOULD TRY THAT

Although you follow Feng Sh*t, you're still allowed to collect an inordinate number of cleaner, polish, and detergent bottles in one of your kitchen cabinets.

WHAT'S ON?

Keep last week's *TV Guide* floating around the living room as well as this week's.

HELLO, DARLINGS

Teach the kids to dump their school bags and
lunch boxes wherever they want.

DID YOU HAVE
A NICE DAY?

At the same time, teach the kids to dump their
coats, hats, gloves, homework folders, and
library books wherever they want.

"WHY SHOULD I DO IT WHEN YOU DON'T, MOMMY?"

Finally, instill in your children the value of
never putting the video cassettes back in the
right cases.

MUST WRITE THOSE DOWN SOMEWHERE

Because it's the only record you have of your nephew's birthday and your wedding anniversary, keep last year's calendar stuffed behind the telephone.

ORGANIZED CHAOS

Buy a large wicker tray or basket and make it your "Things Pending" pile. Quietly feed and nurture it until its contents start to spill onto the surrounding table or shelf. Tend to its contents only in emergency situations–before dinner parties, or when vital pieces of household documentation are lost.

THE 3-STEP RUBBISH PLAN

1. Buy trash bags that are fractionally too small for your trash can.

2. Rather than empty the can, squash down the contents so that more trash will fit.

3. Keep squashing in more trash until you are confident the bag will split when you do lift it out.

POTPOURRI

Buy lots of it. It categorically does nothing
except collect dust.

WHEN THERE'S NOTHING
MUCH TO DO ON A SUNDAY

Go to a few garage sales:
to buy more junk, not sell yours, of course.

114

GET THE BIGGEST ONE

When ordering pizza always get the largest size; then the pizza box won't fit in the garbage can and will lie beside it on the kitchen floor for several days instead.

BONUS: It makes a great ashtray.

COLOR CODING

If your bathroom sink is white, use blue
toothpaste. The build-up of toothpaste scum
will be noticeable much sooner.

FILL IN THIS SURVEY AND YOU MIGHT WIN $10,000!

Always resolve to fill in the lengthy consumer
surveys that arrive in the junk mail.
While you don't get around to it,
it can lie on the kitchen table with
everything else.

HMM, I CAN'T THINK OF A SINGLE GOOD REASON TO KEEP THESE

Your *Rough Guide* and *Lonely Planet* guidebooks are eight years out of date, and you're unlikely to ever travel to Russia, Brazil, or China again, but this does *not* give you licence to throw them away.

BECAUSE FINANCIAL INSTITUTIONS CANNOT BE TRUSTED

Keep every single bank statement, checkbook stub, and credit card bill, dating back from your sixteenth birthday—in a shoebox.

BE EASILY IMPRESSED

Put into practice the handy hints you read in the paper or see on TV, like keeping all your old stockings to tie up shrubs and tomatoes– no matter how irrelevant they may be to your own lifestyle.

A WINDOW CLEANING FABLE

*Once upon a time there was a wise old man,
who said: "If you live in a cold, damp climate,
you shall receive enough rain and condensation
to rinse all dust and grime off your window
panes. If you live in a warm, dry climate,
your windows shall be open most of the time,
so to clean them would have little
consequence upon your view."*
So do not bother cleaning your windows.

IT MIGHT BE WORTH SOMETHING SOME DAY

Live in the false hope that if you keep all your phone cards, postcards and cartoon character bubblebath bottles, they might one day be of value on "Antiques Roadshow."

CAR SH*T

To some people, your car will provide their first introduction to your personal standards. To promote your excellent Feng Sh*t skills, you must ensure your car is a complete disaster at all times. If you've read this much of the book, it shouldn't be too difficult.

INVASION OF THE FLUORESCENT SQUARE

Buy Post-It® Notes in multipacks and operate
all ten pads simultaneously.

WHEN ALL ELSE FAILS

Take out a whopping big loan and build an
addition to your house. Fortunately, all Feng
Sh*t associated with an addition generally
comes free of charge.

FENG SH*T VOCABULARY

Usage examples of key words and phrases:

avoid = "I didn't see it!"

delay = "I'll do it later!"

delegate = "You do it!"

can't = "I don't know how!"

pig-headed = "I don't care!"

EXECUTIVE SUMMARY:
FENG SH*T IN
FIVE EASY STEPS

Take shortcuts.

Adore *things*: they make clutter.

Have inadequate storage.

Be disorganized.

Hoard with religious zeal.

NOTA BENE

There is a subtle but crucial difference
between sh*t and filth. Always challenge your
boundaries but never cross the threshold.
Filth is disgusting!

ABOUT THE AUTHOR

Born and raised in New Zealand, Anna Crosbie now lives in England with her husband and two sons.

She would like to stress that her Dear Mother is in no way responsible for the habits promoted in this book.